"Sacred and Great"

"SACRED AND GREAT"

A Brief Introduction to the
Traditional Latin Mass

by Joseph Shaw

Os Justi
Press

Lincoln, Nebraska

A longer version of this booklet is available from the
Catholic Truth Society, under the title *How to Attend
the Extraordinary Form*. The content here is used with
permission.

Os Justi Press
P.O. Box 21814
Lincoln, NE 68542
https://osjustipress.com/

Inquiries to
info@osjustipress.com

Paperback ISBN 978-1-960711-12-0
eBook ISBN 978-1-960711-13-7

Interior design: Nora Malone
Cover design: Julian Kwasniewski

CONTENTS

INTRODUCTION

Perhaps you've been once or twice to a celebration of the older form of the Catholic liturgy—usually called the "Traditional Latin Mass" (TLM)—because it happened to be at a convenient time on a Sunday. Perhaps someone brought you to see it, or you were curious about it yourself, especially after it kept coming up in the news. Perhaps you came into a church where it was being celebrated, quite by chance. Perhaps you've never attended it, but have heard about it.

For Catholics used to the newer form of the Mass, the Novus Ordo, experiencing the older one raises a lot of questions. Why has the priest got his back to me? Why is everything in Latin? Is this kind of Mass even allowed? Most urgently: how am I supposed to participate in this liturgy? How can it be spiritually fruitful for me?

This booklet has been written to answer these questions, or as many of them as possible. It will be a brief answer; those who wish to read more are directed to the "Further Reading and Resources" at the end.

This booklet has been written by a layman, from the perspective of the laity. Like nearly all cradle Catholics in the Western Church today, I was brought up with the Novus Ordo Mass, celebrated in my mother tongue, and I didn't discover the traditional Mass until my late twenties. It is the astonishment felt at that moment of discovery, whether one views it positively, or with concern, or just with confusion, that this booklet is designed to address.

The traditional Mass is the "classical," the central and historically most widespread, form of Mass in the Western Church. For centuries it was attended by kings, soldiers, merchants, peasants, and children. It formed saints and scholars, converted sinners, sustained monks and nuns, inspired martyrs, and comforted the afflicted, in a complete range of social and economic conditions: from the basilicas of ancient Rome to the battlefields of the Second World War; from the mission stations of Africa, to the suffering Church in Communist China. Nothing should stop you engaging fruitfully with it, as they did.

How Do I Participate in the Traditional Mass?

A glimpse of heaven

This booklet starts at the end: not with the history of
the Mass, or the symbolic significance of its individual
ceremonies, but with how to participate in it. The question of participation arises from the experience of the
traditional Mass, an experience that is somewhat different from the experience of the Novus Ordo.

It may be a busy church or an empty one, and it
may be a Low Mass or a Sung Mass (terms that will be
explained below), but the impression created by the
traditional Mass for a worshipper used to the Novus
Ordo is distinctive. The Mass is taking place in the
sanctuary: the priest bows before the Altar, engages
in a dialogue with the server, and proceeds to perform
a series of prayers and ceremonies at the Altar. There
may be singing going on, but it is not led by the priest,
and he doesn't in general appear to take any notice

of it, but continues with the Mass while it goes on. Members of the congregation may take part in some of the singing, and may make some responses, but except when he preaches, the priest does not even look at them. Many of the ceremonies are partially hidden from view, since the priest is facing away from the nave. Some of the words are said so quietly that even the server kneeling next to the celebrant can hardly hear them. The ones said aloud are in Latin.

Mass seems to be happening *over there*, in some place set apart from the congregation, and without the congregation's visible involvement. How to understand and engage with it is the central practical question for those new to attending the traditional Mass.

If you feel that you are being excluded, in a certain sense you are correct. We in the nave of the church are on the outside of something, but all the same we are looking in. We are, in fact, catching a glimpse of the heavenly liturgy. As the scholar Fr Michel Sinoir writes, noting the parallel with the liturgy of the Eastern Churches:

> The [Eastern] iconostasis symbolically is Heaven, and its liturgy, which anticipates Heaven, is

celebrated only by members of the clergy. The nave is symbolically the earth, the abode of men and women who are preparing themselves to enter into Glory. This is by analogy the same mystery as that of Christ-the-Bridegroom, renewing in the sanctuary His sacrifice, which is gratefully received by the Church-His-Bride who is still in pilgrimage here below.[1]

In this way, attending the traditional Mass can be understood as the privilege of seeing, from a distance, something of great solemnity and holiness. The things that contribute to the distance between the priest (and his doings) and the congregation are essential to creating the corresponding sense of the sacred. The fact that we can't see things clearly because the priest has his back to us; the use of Latin; silent prayers; the exclusion of the laity from the sanctuary, except for vested servers: all these things serve to remind us that we are looking in at something very special, from the outside.

---

[1] Fr Michel Sinoir, *La question de l'admission des femmes au service de l'autel* (Paris: Pierre Téqui, 1994), 26; trans. Fr Brian Harrison.

The distance here is not a distance of *understanding*. We can, if we wish, learn all about the ceremonies and prayers; those who learn to serve Mass must do so. We can follow all the texts in a hand missal. Even without doing either of those things, a Catholic attending Mass can, should, and usually does know what is going on, in general terms—it is the Sacrifice of the Mass—and in specific terms—the significance of each part of the Mass.

There is a distance all the same. It is the distance between heaven and earth, between what is holy and set apart, and what is profane, the everyday world: not between the good and the bad, but between the supernatural and the natural. By acknowledging the reality of the distance between heavenly and earthly things, the traditional Mass allows us to witness, to experience, heavenly things, and not only to experience them, but to unite ourselves with them. In other words, by representing, symbolically and dramatically, the chasm that separates us mortals from the things of God, the TLM makes it possible to bridge that chasm.

To repeat, the TLM marks off the holiness of holy things: they are separated from us, and from all ordinary things. The sanctuary is separated from the nave;

the language used is separate from the language of everyday speech; the type of music is a distinct, sacred style; the vestments of the priest are equally special, separate, and sacred. The point of all this is not to keep us away, however, but to draw us in. We can see and hear this special zone, and we unite ourselves to it by our prayer, because we unite our intentions and our prayers to those of the priest celebrating the Mass.

This is spiritual participation in the Mass. By uniting ourselves with something that is palpably holy, it is able to enter *us*, to transform us, as happens in a special way when we receive Holy Communion.

The Catholic religion contains something astonishing and awe-inspiring: the real and living presence of Christ in the Blessed Sacrament on the Altar, and the Sacrifice Christ made of Himself on Mount Calvary, offered in an unbloody manner in the Mass. Somehow the liturgy of the Mass must impress on the people both that the Mass is what the Faith tells us it is, and also that we are invited to take part in these things. It is not so much a balance that needs to be struck as a paradox that needs to be emphasised. Yes, it is a fearful thing to be in the presence of God. And yes, we may remain there, sinners as we are, and take part in the Church's own worship of God, which, because it is Christ's prayer and offering, is a perfect worship, acceptable to God. The traditional Mass does this precisely by letting the holiness and otherness of what is taking place, and of what is present, take precedence and stand forth visibly and palpably. It is the *holy nature* of these things that we are invited first to acknowledge, and then to partake in.

Pope Francis expressed it, in addressing a Russian journalist about the liturgy of the Eastern Churches, in this way:

> In the Orthodox Churches, they have retained that pristine liturgy, which is so beautiful. We have lost some of the sense of adoration. The Orthodox preserved it; they praise God, they adore God, they sing, time does not matter. God is at the center, and I would like to say, as you ask me this question, that this is a richness.[2]

Here Pope Francis himself makes the parallel between the Eastern Liturgy and the Western liturgy before

---

[2] Apostolic Journey to Rio de Janeiro on the Occasion of the XXVIII World Youth Day: Press Conference of Pope Francis during the Return Flight, Sunday, July 28, 2013.

the Second Vatican Council, which, for most Western Catholics, has been "lost." This loss is not absolute, however: the sense of adoration and the centrality of God can still be experienced at the traditional Mass.

Practical advice

To participate in Mass means something specific: to unite our prayers with those of the priest, and to offer ourselves to God, together with the offering of Christ by the priest. Some of the prayers of the Mass refer to this: for example, when the priest speaks of the offering of "my sacrifice and yours," two, distinct, offerings are referred to.

Again, our attendance at Mass is an opportunity to bring to God any specific intentions we may have, whether they be our own needs, those of others, or loved ones who have died. Mass is offered for "the living and the dead."[3]

Nevertheless, the precise way we prayerfully participate in Mass is left open to us, and in the traditional Mass the laity are given considerable freedom. Prayer, the Church teaches us, is the lifting up of the mind and

---

[3] *Roman Pontifical,* formula used during the ordination of a priest.

heart to God,[4] and this can be done in many ways. We can do it by following the prayers of the Mass in a hand missal; we can say other appropriate prayers, which may be found in devotional books; we can say other formal prayers, such as the Rosary; or we can simply contemplate the action of the Mass in a recollected way, knowing what we are witnessing and uniting ourselves with it.

In 1964, the novelist Evelyn Waugh wrote: " 'Participation' in the Mass does not mean hearing our own voices. It means God hearing our voices. Only He knows who is 'participating' at Mass. I believe, to compare small things with great, that I 'participate' in a work of art when I study it and love it silently. No need to shout."[5]

Earlier, Pope Pius XII, having mentioned methods of participation such as reading the prayers of the Mass in a hand missal, added:

> The needs and inclinations of all are not the same, nor are they always constant in the same individual. Who, then, would say, on account

---

[4]   See the *Penny Catechism* 141.
[5]   Letter to the Editor of *The Catholic Herald*, August 7, 1964, reproduced in *A Bitter Trial*, expanded ed., ed. Alcuin Reid (San Francisco: Ignatius Press, 2011), 57.

of such a prejudice, that all these Christians [who are not following word-for-word] cannot participate in the Mass nor share its fruits? On the contrary, they can adopt some other method which proves easier for certain people; for instance, they can lovingly meditate on the mysteries of Jesus Christ or perform other exercises of piety or recite prayers which, though they differ from the sacred rites, are still essentially in harmony with them.[6]

As Pope Pius indicated, those who attend the traditional Mass regularly will find that different methods of directing their participation appeal to them on different occasions, depending on their mood and circumstances.

Broadly speaking, the structure of the Mass is the same in the traditional Mass as in the Novus Ordo, but there are a number of differences that can be confusing. If you are going to attend regularly, it makes sense to look at a booklet of the "Ordinary of the Mass" (the fixed prayers) to see what is going on at each stage. This can be done at Mass, or outside of Mass. You may want

---

[6] Pope Pius XII, Encyclical Letter *Mediator Dei* (1947), no. 108.

to learn more from liturgical commentaries, some of which are listed in the Further Reading and Resources section. Hand missals provide all the texts of the Mass, including the variable parts. Today, many of these resources are available as apps on smart phones.

Equally, however, no one should feel a slave to a missal: on occasion, a missal can even feel like a distraction from the Mass. For those new to the Mass, some may find it best simply to experience the liturgy, without the mediation of printed texts. Above all, allow the Mass to speak to you in its own way.

Different kinds of traditional Mass

It may be helpful to explain briefly the different kinds of traditional Mass.

The key distinction is based on the liturgical resources available for a particular Mass. A "Low" Mass can be celebrated by a priest with one or two servers, or at a pinch with no server. The ceremonies are necessarily simpler than in other forms of Mass, although it might be better to say that the ceremonies are *compressed*, which gives them a certain heightened intensity.

Especially with a small congregation, and perhaps in a small chapel, it can be very quiet, low-key, and intimate, as well as relatively short, which makes it very practical as a Mass to be said or attended before or after a day's work, or in a lunch break.

If singers are available, to sing both the chants of the day and the "ordinary" chants (Kyrie, Gloria, Credo, Sanctus, Agnus Dei), then Mass can be sung. In its fullest form, this is the *Missa Solemnis*, the "Solemn High" Mass: this requires the assistance of a deacon and a subdeacon in addition to the celebrating priest. It involves a number of very beautiful ceremonies that aren't seen at other forms of the Mass, such as the "Pax" (kiss of peace), and the proclamation of the Gospel away from the altar, with candles and incense. Because of the need for extra clergy, this is relatively less common.

There is also an intermediate form, *Missa Cantata*, called the "Sung" or "High" Mass. This does not require a deacon or subdeacon, but it does need singers. It can be (and nearly always is) celebrated with incense, but if there aren't enough servers available it can be celebrated without incense and just one or two servers. The ceremonies are a compromise between those of Low Mass and those of Solemn Mass. Sung Masses like this tend to be celebrated on Sundays and important feasts wherever the traditional Mass is well established.

The Mass for the Dead, used at funerals and on the anniversaries of loved ones, has certain unique features. For example, the prayers said by the priest and servers at the beginning of the Mass are shorter, and there may be a ceremony of sprinkling of holy water at the end of Mass, not only if a body is present prior to a burial service, but of an empty coffin or coffin-stand, representing those for whom the Mass is offered. It can be celebrated as a Low, Sung, or Solemn Mass.

The reverent and restrained qualities of the traditional "Requiem" Mass, as it is called (the opening chant begins "Requiem aeternam," "eternal rest"), makes it specially suitable for Masses celebrated for the deceased. It includes, among many very beautiful chants, the *Dies Irae*, which must count as one of the most influential pieces of music of any age or genre.

The Requiem's musical texts can be sung to polyphonic settings composed by some of the greatest Catholic musicians of history, as well as to their ancient chant settings. This distinction applies to all sung Masses, although polyphonic composers tended not to compose the chants of the day for Sunday and feastday

Masses, but only the ordinary chants, so Masses where polyphony is sung will usually also have Gregorian chant as well.

Polyphonic musical settings require singers with different voices—most often four, soprano, alto, bass, and tenor—and exist for all periods of music, from the earliest polyphonic music of the Renaissance, to Classical and modern music. Gregorian chant has also been composed over many centuries, when new feasts have been created, but the core repertoire dates from between the eighth and tenth centuries. Both can be heard on occasion in the Novus Ordo, but at the traditional Mass they are heard more frequently, because the liturgical law does not allow them to be replaced by hymns in sung Masses.

A note on posture during Mass

Those new to the traditional Mass may notice the people doing more kneeling than in the Novus Ordo. A more fundamental difference, however, is that whereas rules are laid down for the people's postures in the newer Mass, in the TLM it is a matter of personal preference and local custom, and there is in practice a bit of variation between congregations.

All congregations stand for the Gospel and kneel for the Consecration. For the rest of Mass you can suit yourself, with due respect for local practice, and what may inconvenience or distract others. The instructions given in missals or handouts (which themselves vary) should be regarded as suggestions, not hard and fast rules.

The tone and ethos of the traditional Mass

It was noted above that the traditional Mass impresses us with a sense of the sacred. It is useful to note the means it uses, and does not use, to do this.

Some find the idea of a Mass entirely in Latin, with or without complex musical accompaniment, intimidating. It should be stressed, therefore, that in reality the traditional Mass actually leaves us to our own thoughts to a surprising extent: as noted above, it is possible to say one's own prayers during it, as well as to follow all the texts in a missal. It is not bombastic or demanding. If we consider its texts, the traditional architecture and fittings of a church, traditional vestments, and above all, the form of sacred music specially developed to serve it—Gregorian chant—there is nothing that judges us, bullies or harangues us, or seeks to overwhelm us with sentimentality.

Pope Pius X insisted on Gregorian chant, and those forms of music most akin to it, as most appropriate to the liturgy,[7] and his words were echoed by the Second Vatican Council.[8] In the chant and in the texts and ceremonies of the Mass, the liturgy has a great emotional range, from penance and grief, to expectation and joy, but this is expressed with a great economy of means, and without emotional manipulation.

The predictability and steadiness of the ancient liturgy gives the more dramatic moments, for example during the ceremonies of Holy Week, special force, just as the silence of the central prayers of the Mass accords a greater impact to the ringing of the bell for the consecration. The language of the prayers is restrained, and yet insistent.

Ceremonies, chants, and the use of silence as well as the spoken word, enable the liturgy to enter

---

[7] Pope Pius X, *Tra la Sollecitudini* (1907), no. 3.
[8] Second Vatican Council, Constitution on the Liturgy *Sacrosanctum Concilium* (1962), no. 116.

the worshipper not only at the intellectual level. As Pope John Paul II noted of the traditional liturgy of the Eastern Churches, which have much in common with that of the Western Church: "The lengthy duration of the celebrations, the repeated invocations, everything expresses gradual identification with the mystery celebrated with one's whole person."[9]

The venerable age of the traditional Mass is another aspect of its ethos. It connects us today with the Catholics of every century, back to the times of the early Church, the Age of the Fathers. Popes, Doctors, and Saints prayed the very same words, and listened to the same readings, and many of the things they said about the Mass make sense in the context of the traditional Mass as celebrated today.[10] This unity, through time as well as space, gives a special sense of solidarity with our predecessors in the Faith when we participate in the TLM.

The overall effect of the tone and ethos of the traditional Mass is that of *peace.* When we attend the

---

[9] Pope John Paul II, Apostolic Letter *Orientale Lumen* (1995), no. 11.

[10] See Thomas Crean, *The Mass and the Saints* (San Francisco: Ignatius Press, 2008).

traditional Mass we leave the noisy and busy world, and enter a timeless oasis of calm. In this way it gives great consolation to those attached to it, and it does not make demands upon us at odds with the feelings we may have: our stress, exhaustion, grief, or, for that matter, our joy. For many people, the TLM is, in its own words (speaking of heaven), "a place of refreshment, light, and peace": *locus refrigerii, lucis et pacis.*[11]

---

[11] The phrase occurs in the Roman Canon.

2

WHAT DOES IT MEAN?
Ceremonies and Prayers

In this chapter a number of specific issues about Mass celebrated in the traditional rite will be addressed. They have been chosen principally because they are the issues that those new to this form of Mass most often find surprising, rather than because they are the most important aspects of the Mass.[12] What is most important of all, in the Mass, are things the traditional Mass has in common with the Novus Ordo: the Sacrifice and the Sacrament. The following discussion will take for granted a degree of familiarity with Mass in itself, to address what is different about the TLM.

---

[12] A fuller treatment of a larger number of such issues can be found in Joseph Shaw, ed., *The Case for Liturgical Restoration* (Brooklyn: Angelico Press, 2019).

"Ad orientem": facing East

One of the most immediately striking features of the traditional Mass is the way the priest faces away from the people for nearly all of the Mass. The Novus Ordo can be celebrated like this, "*ad orientem*," but this is rare.

The practice is called *ad orientem* because the priest is facing the direction of the rising sun (from the Latin "*oriens*," for "rising"). Until the sixteenth century churches were usually built with the altar at their geographical east end, but even when this is not the case, we can talk about "liturgical east": what is symbolically regarded as the east. In any case, in the practice of the traditional Mass, the priest faces the same direction as the people, towards the crucifix.

The psychological impact of this arrangement is considerable, because it makes immediately clear that the priest is not addressing himself to the congregation, except for the moments in the Mass when he turns around specifically to do so. The dramatic distinction between these moments and the rest of the Mass underlines the reality that the Mass is an act of worship directed towards God, and not something directed towards the people. In this act of worship, the priest is united with the people, leading them in prayer: the priest is *with* the people, representing the people before God, rather than, as it were, coming from a different direction, and facing them.

Another effect of worship *ad orientem* is to minimise the significance of the priest as an individual. For much of the Mass we cannot see his face, and even when he does turn around, the rubrics instruct him to keep his eyes lowered. There is therefore no eye-contact, no expression of the priest's personality, and no reliance on his personal charisma, to engage the congregation. In the absence of those things, we are reminded that the priest celebrates Mass not as himself, but *in persona Christi*: Christ acts through him so completely that he is able to say the words of Christ, at the Consecration, as if they were his own: "This is my Body. . . . This is the chalice of my Blood. . . . Do this in memory of Me."

The importance of *ad orientem* celebration was particularly championed in the theological writings of Joseph Ratzinger, before his election as Pope Benedict XVI. He was concerned that worship *"versus populum"* (facing the people) could lead to a community becoming closed in on itself. He wrote:

Looking at the priest has no importance. What matters is looking together at the Lord. It is not now a question of dialogue, but of common worship, of setting off towards the One who is to come. What corresponds with the reality of what is happening is not the closed circle, but the common movement forward expressed in a common direction for prayer.[13]

The reference to "the One who is to come" relates to the reason for the choice of east as the common direction. The east represents the Second Coming of Christ, as indicated in Matthew 24:27: "For as lightning cometh out of the east, and appeareth even unto the west: so shall the coming of the Son of man be."[14] This means that a common, eastward, direction of worship is given an eschatological dimension. Mass does not only look back to the Crucifixion, but forward to Christ's return in glory.

---

[13] Joseph Ratzinger, *The Spirit of the Liturgy* (San Francisco: Ignatius Press, 2000), 81.

[14] Related texts include Zechariah 3:8, Malachi 3:30, John 1:9, Psalm 67:34.

Although, as noted, celebration of the Novus Ordo *ad orientem* is rare, the issue itself was not addressed at the Second Vatican Council, and, as illustrated by the writings of Joseph Ratzinger and Cardinal Sarah (among many others), it remains a sorely debated liturgical issue. The practice of worship *ad orientem* is also used by the Eastern Churches, and the suggestion that they adopt the now usual Western practice has been strongly resisted by the Congregation for the Eastern Churches:

> It is not a question, as is often claimed, of presiding the celebration with the back turned towards the people, but rather of guiding the people in pilgrimage toward the Kingdom, invoked in prayer until the return of the Lord. Such practice . . . is thus of profound value and should be safeguarded. . . .[15]

Silence

Another immediately striking thing about the traditional Mass is the silence. Almost the whole of the

---

[15] Instruction *Il Padre, incomprensibile* (1996), 107.

Canon (the Eucharistic Prayer), and a number of other prayers, are said by the priest so quietly that they cannot be heard. This is related to another contrast between the two Forms, which is that at Sung Masses, singing by the choir continues over certain parts of the Mass in the TLM, whereas in the Novus Ordo the priest's proclamation of the liturgical texts more often has to wait until any singing has finished.

The silence of the most important part of the Mass, including the words of Consecration, distinguishes it from what precedes and follows it, and marks it off as something particularly special. When Mass is sung, there is singing before and after, by the priest and by the choir (the Preface and the *Sanctus* before, and the *Pater Noster* and the *Agnus Dei* after). Singing is one way of giving a text greater prominence and solemnity. To go beyond this, to show that the solemnity of the Mass has risen to a yet higher level, there is silence. It signals that we have arrived at a point where, for the congregation, words no longer suffice. For the priest, it is the point where he must commune, alone, with God, as when the High Priest of the Jewish Temple passed behind the curtain into the Holy of Holies: "the Lord is in his holy temple. Let all the earth keep silence before him."[16] And again, it recalls the silence of the Crucifixion.

Of all the aspects of the traditional Mass that we can isolate—and of course, they really do their work in combination—it is silence whose effectiveness in assisting the Faithful can be most clearly experienced. Those who have not experienced it may find it hard to imagine, but during the silence of the Canon of the Mass one can become oddly detached even from the noise of people digging up the road outside, or of small children in the congregation. It is not, after all, a silence indicating that nothing is happening, but a silence of intense and deep activity. As Joseph Ratzinger, to quote him again, expressed it:

> Anyone who has experienced a church united in the silent praying of the Canon will know what a really *filled* silence is. It is at once a loud and penetrating cry to God and a Spirit-filled act of prayer. Here everyone does pray the Canon together, albeit in a bond with the special task of the priestly ministry. Here everyone is united,

---

[16] Habakkuk 2:20.

laid hold of by Christ, and led by the Holy Spirit
into that common prayer to the Father which
is the true sacrifice—the love that reconciles
and unites God and the world.[17]

This silence powerfully stimulates the worshipper to contemplative prayer, and its value is heightened, rather than diminished, by the insistent noise
of modern life. As Pope John Paul II wrote, on the
role of silence in the liturgy: "In a society that lives at
an increasingly frenetic pace, often deafened by noise
and confused by the ephemeral, it is vital to rediscover
the value of silence."[18]

We may say, indeed, that silence is God's language.
As Pope Benedict XVI wrote: "If God speaks to us even
in silence, we in turn discover in silence the possibil-
ity of speaking with God and about God. We need
that silence which becomes contemplation, which
introduces us into God's silence and brings us to the
point where the Word, the redeeming Word, is born."[19]

---

[17] Ratzinger, *The Spirit of the Liturgy*, 215–16.

[18] Pope John Paul II, Apostolic Letter *Spiritus et Sponsa* (2003).

[19] Pope Benedict XVI, Message for the 46th World Communi-
cations Day: "Silence and the Word: Path of Evangelization"
(2012).

Latin

In light of the role of silence in the traditional Mass, it is less surprising that the rest of the Mass is celebrated in a special language, Latin. If one need not even *hear* the most important part of the Mass in order to participate in it with special intensity, then it follows that one need not understand, at a word-by-word level, other parts of the Mass, to participate in them.

As noted in Chapter 1, neither the inaudibility nor the use of Latin in practice creates a barrier of understanding between the worshipper and the liturgy, since members of the congregation can consult a hand missal, printout, or smart phone, to see exactly what is being said, translated into a wide variety of languages. What it does do is to mark off the liturgy as something special and distinct from ordinary life. When we enter into the Latin zone, so to speak, we are entering into a spiritual space.

In this way Latin powerfully reinforces the atmosphere created by the architecture and fittings of a church building, the special vestments worn by the clergy, the distinct type of music appropriate to the Mass, and so on. The 2011 English translation of the Mass followed guidelines set out in the Instruction

Liturgiam Authenticam, which called for a "sacred style that will come to be recognised as proper to liturgical language."[20] The use of Latin takes this principle a step further. In the Western Church, the liturgical language *par excellence* is Latin.

Latin long ago ceased to be the cradle language of any particular community, a fact that strengthens its role as a universal sacred language for the many language-communities that make up the Western Church—a role increasingly useful for the multilingual parishes now found in many parts of the world, and for travellers.

The Latin of the Mass was never, in truth, the language of the street, or of the public speaker. Not only is it often flowery and poetic, but it is strongly marked by the influence of Greek and Hebrew, and makes extensive use of repetition and deliberate archaism. It was always intended to be what it is: a distinct, holy, language, to be used only in the liturgy.[21]

---

[20] Congregation for Divine Worship, Instruction *Liturgiam Authenticam* (2001), no. 27.

[21] See Christine Mohrmann, *Liturgical Latin: Its Origins and Character* (Washington, DC: Catholic University of America Press, 1957).

Pope Paul VI, who authorised Mass to be celebrated in vernacular languages, nevertheless remarked in 1966 that liturgical Latin was "an abundant wellspring of Christian civilisation and a very rich treasure-trove of devotion." In 1969, he told a General Audience: "The introduction of the vernacular will certainly be a great sacrifice for those who know the beauty, the power, and the expressive sacrality of Latin. We are parting with the speech of the Christian centuries; we are becoming like profane intruders in the literary preserve of sacred utterance." Again, he refers to "that language of the angels," "the divine Latin language."

It would seem that Pope Paul felt that his own appreciation of Latin was characteristic of an educational elite. It is certainly true that learning Latin and becoming familiar with the Latin of the Vulgate (the version of the Bible usually used in the traditional Mass) brings great rewards, in opening up the poetic qualities of the liturgy, and its frequent scriptural references. It has become evident, however, that the Latin liturgy is appreciated by many whose knowledge of Latin is limited or nonexistent.

The explanation for this has already been indicated: as a marker of the sacred, it enables us to enter into the spirit of the liturgy more fully. As Pope John Paul II remarked: "There are also those people who, having been educated on the basis of the old liturgy in Latin, experience the lack of this 'one language,' which in all the world was an expression of the unity of the Church and through its dignified character elicited a profound sense of the Eucharistic Mystery."[22]

One does not have to understand the Latin text word by word as it is spoken, to perceive the solemn character with which it clothes the liturgy, and to be moved by that. The meaning of the text can be immediately available to the worshipper in a book or leaflet, but the impact the *form* the text takes, the fact that it is proclaimed in an ancient, sacred language, of unique grandeur and gravity, is also of considerable value.

This is something well understood by Christians in the Eastern Churches, most of whom use special, sacred languages for the liturgy, whether it be an archaic form of Greek, Church Slavonic in Russia, or Ge'ez in Ethiopia. The same is true of many non-Christian

---

[22] Pope John Paul II, Apostolic Letter *Dominicae Cenae* (1980), no. 10.

religions: non-Arab-speaking Muslims pray in classical Arabic, and Hindus, Buddhists, and Jains, in Sanskrit. It would, in fact, be a strange thing if Western Christianity alone had no sacred language of its own.

The repeated liturgical use of Latin does, in fact, establish a familiarity over time that enables the worshipper not only to recognize what part of the Mass is taking place (the *Gloria*, for example, or the *Agnus Dei*), but to know the fixed prayers of the Mass well enough to understand them as they are proclaimed in Latin. As noted in Chapter 1, it makes sense to familiarise yourself with the Mass with a translation to hand. Soon, many key Latin words will become familiar.

The lectionary

The differences between the Lectionaries of the Novus Ordo and the traditional Mass are not so striking to the ordinary Mass-goer as the issues just dealt with, but the topic is included because it is sometimes said, even by those sympathetic to the TLM, that the older Lectionary is clearly deficient by comparison with the reformed one. The reason for this is that, with its multi-year cycle and additional reading on Sundays, the revised Lectionary includes more Scripture. The rationale of the Lectionary in the traditional Mass accordingly demands some explanation.

At each TLM there is (with a few exceptions) just one non-Gospel reading, and a reading from the Gospel. There are readings assigned for each Sunday and important feastday of the year, for every day of Lent, and for Votive Masses. Less important saints' days have readings (and other "proper" texts, such as the Collect) from the "Commons of the Saints," a few of which exist for each category of saint: Pope, Doctor, Martyr, Holy Woman, and so on. The net result is that a regular worshipper at the traditional Mass will in time become familiar with the Sunday gospels, and a weekday Mass-goer will even more quickly begin to recognise the readings given for many of the saints: the Confession of St Peter (Mt 16:13–19) for the popes; the description of the "valiant woman" (Prov 31) for holy women; the story of the woman in the crowd praising the Blessed Virgin Mary (Lk 11:27–28), for many of her Votive Masses. These readings are often related to, and sometimes quoted in, the other texts of the day.

One consequence of this system is that the readings and prayers of each day's Mass always pertain to the feast of the day, instead of simply being the readings that come after the readings of the previous day.[23] On Sundays, the TLM's readings form a series that relates to the season, working up to a climax of eschatological expectation, most notably, just before, and at the beginning of, Advent, and giving advice on penance before and during Lent. Without going into technical details, this kind of festal or seasonal pertinence is more difficult to achieve with the "*lectio continua*" ("continuous reading") principle that governs the Lectionary of the Novus Ordo.

The appropriateness of the readings to the day, and the people's greater familiarity with a smaller set of readings, have something to be said for them: there is loss as well as gain with the larger set of readings provided in the Novus Ordo. Curiously, the much larger, reformed Lectionary also omits some of the passages used in the older Lectionary, and this points

---

[23] It is true that the Novus Ordo *permits* readings to be taken from one or another "common of saints" in the lectionary; but the rubrical instructions seem to discourage this apart from special occasions, encouraging rather the *lectio continua* or the maintenance of the ongoing daily cycle.

to another aspect of the contrast between the modern Mass and the traditional Mass.

The omitted passages are generally those that were regarded, when the new Lectionary was being developed in the late 1960s, as in some sense "difficult." The prophet Daniel's vision of the Abomination of Desolation in the Temple is not referred to in the readings of the Novus Ordo, either in the Gospels, or in the Old Testament;[24] nor is Jesus's warning that his disciples would be ejected from the Synagogues,[25] or St Paul's admonition to the Corinthians to receive Holy Communion with a clear conscience:[26] examples could be multiplied. Similarly, the proper and the ordinary prayers of the Missal were carefully edited by the reformers to remove references and themes that they thought could be off-putting to modern people.

The net result is that in attending the traditional Mass one is far more often brought up short by aspects of Scripture and Tradition that otherwise receive less attention: the realities of persecution, the hostility of

---

[24] Matthew 24:15–35; Mark 13:14ff.; Daniel 9:27, 11:31, 12:11; 1 Machabees 1:57.
[25] John 16:1–4.
[26] 1 Corinthians 11:27–29.

"the world," our sinfulness and need for contrition and penance, divine punishment, and God's grace. There is a certain brutal honesty about it: things are not being swept under the carpet. Whether one is sated with the unsatisfying sweetness of consumerism, or suffering under the harsher side of modern life, the astringent quality of the traditional Mass can serve as a useful corrective, and even a relief.

Liturgical seasons and the calendar

The issue of liturgical seasons is included here mainly because it is a potential source of confusion. Christmas and Easter obviously fall on the same days in the Novus Ordo and the traditional Mass, but there are also a number of differences.

The most important is the season of three Sundays preceding Lent, during which the celebrant wears violet. This is a season of preparation for Lent, called "Septuagesima," as it starts (roughly) 70 days before Easter.

Since Lent is itself a preparation for Easter, getting ready for Lent might seem redundant, but it does have its uses. A season of penance benefits from some preparation, no less than a season of celebration. Mgr (later,

Archbishop) Annibale Bugnini, the Vatican official who was responsible for the abolition of Septuagesima, records an interesting defence of it by Pope Paul VI:

> On one occasion Pope Paul VI compared the complex made up of Septuagesima, Lent, Holy Week and Easter Triduum, to the bells calling people to Sunday Mass. The ringing of them an hour, a half-hour, fifteen and five minutes before the time of Mass has a psychological effect and prepares the faithful materially and spiritually for the celebration of the liturgy.[27]

From a practical point of view, it can serve to remind us to decide in good time what form our Lenten penance should take: what to "give up," or what extra devotions or good works to adopt.

In a somewhat similar way, the calendar of the traditional Mass has more days on which an important feast is prepared for, or celebrated. The season of Christmas is longer, lasting until the feast of the Presentation on February 2; Pentecost has an "octave,"

---

[27] Annibale Bugnini, *The Reform of the Liturgy 1948–1975* (Collegeville, MN: The Liturgical Press, 1990), 307n6.

being followed by a week of special Masses reminding us of the significance of the coming of the Holy Spirit; a number of important feasts (Christmas Day, the Ascension, the Assumption, and some others) have a "vigil" with its own proper Mass, a day of spiritual preparation for the feast.

The liturgical scholar, Fr Pius Parsch, writing before the Second Vatican Council, gives a practical explanation of octaves, in words that can also be applied to vigils:

> Mother Church is a good psychologist; she understands human nature perfectly. When a feast comes, the soul is amazed and not quite prepared to think profoundly upon its mystery; but on the following days the mind finds it easy to consider the mystery from all sides, sympathetically and deeply; and an eighth day affords a wonderful opportunity to make a synthesis of all points covered.[28]

Considered overall, the calendar of the traditional Mass gives us more contrasts: more days of violet

---

[28] Pius Parsch, *The Church's Year of Grace*, trans. William G. Heidt (Collegeville, MN: The Liturgical Press, 1962), 1:244–45.

vestments with references to fasting, more days of celebration, and also more minor saints' days. This special emphasis on the cult of the saints is also found in regard to the saints in the Confiteor and the Canon, and the way they are handled in the proper prayers. The saints, angels, and Our Lady surround the traditional Mass as our companions and intercessors. This is particularly true of the saints of great antiquity, and this is yet another way the TLM reinforces our communion with the earliest Christian centuries. Saints canonized since 1960 are not included in the old calendar, but a change to the rules in 2020 has made it possible for priests to celebrate the traditional Mass in their honor, without displacing important feasts or saints.

On "free" (ferial) days outside of Lent, priests can choose to celebrate the Mass of the previous Sunday or a Votive Mass, which is an optional Mass for a particular devotion. The Missal recommends some for each day of the week. Mass-goers on ferial weekdays might get a Mass of the Blessed Sacrament, the Sacred Heart, St Joseph, Our Lady on Saturdays, a Mass for the Dead, or one of many others. These Votive Masses are a great boost to the devotion of the Faithful towards these and similar objects. Every day of Lent, on other hand, has its own Mass, which can be superseded only by a feast of some importance.

One might say, as far as the calendar of the traditional Mass goes, that there is always something special going on.

The reception of Communion

An issue of very practical relevance is the way Holy Communion is distributed in the traditional Mass: the Host is given to kneeling communicants (unless illness or disability makes kneeling impossible), and on the tongue, and the communicant does not say "amen." Furthermore, the Precious Blood is not given to the faithful, but consumed only by the celebrant.

Not for the first time in this booklet, Pope Paul VI provides an eloquent defence of a practice that, under him, was almost to disappear. He (or to be exact, the Congregation for Divine Worship under him), wrote in 1969:

> In view of the state of the Church as a whole today, this manner of distributing Holy Communion [on the tongue] must be observed,

not only because it rests upon a tradition of many centuries but especially because it is a sign of the reverence of the faithful toward the Eucharist. The practice in no way detracts from the personal dignity of those who approach this great Sacrament and it is a part of the preparation needed for the most fruitful reception of the Lord's body.

This reverence is a sign of Holy Communion not in "common bread and drink" but in the Body and Blood of the Lord. . . .

In addition, this manner of communicating, which is now to be considered as prescribed by custom, gives more effective assurance that Holy Communion will be distributed with the appropriate reverence, decorum, and dignity; that any danger of profaning the Eucharistic species, in which "the whole and entire Christ, God and man, is substantially contained and permanently present in a unique way," will be avoided; and finally that the diligent care which the Church has always commended for the very fragments of the consecrated bread will be maintained: "If you have allowed anything to be lost, consider this a lessening of your own members."[29]

From the laity's point of view, there can be no doubt that reception on the tongue, together with kneeling, "underscore the Real Presence with an exclamation point,"[30] as Pope Benedict XVI expressed it, when explaining his own decision to insist on this manner of reception in papal celebrations in St Peter's in Rome.

The rationale of placing the Host directly onto the communicant's tongue was explained, at the time of Pope Benedict's decision, by reference to a passage of St Thomas Aquinas: "Out of reverence towards this Sacrament, nothing touches it but what is consecrated; hence the corporal and the chalice are consecrated, and likewise the priest's hands, for touching

---

[29] Congregation for Divine Worship, Instruction *Memoriale Domini* (1969). There are internal quotations and references to St Augustine, St Justin Martyr, the Congregation for Rites, and St Cyril of Jerusalem.

[30] Pope Benedict XVI, *Light of the World: A Conversation with Peter Seewald* (San Francisco: Ignatius Press, 2010) 158–59.

this Sacrament. Hence, it is not lawful for anyone else to touch it except from necessity."[31]

It is interesting to note that, although this manner of receiving the Host took time to develop in the West (and developed in a somewhat different way in the East), the well-known description given by St Cyril of Jerusalem of receiving the Host in the hand in his own day does not involve the communicant picking up the Host with his fingers.[32] Similarly, although in the early centuries communicants received the Precious Blood, this was accompanied by an attitude of great reverence towards the chalice, and communicants were not allowed to touch it, even with their lips.[33] It is the same attitude of concern for holy things, both the Sacred Species and the vessels, which lies behind the practice, of many centuries' duration, of the traditional Mass today.

---

[31] St Thomas Aquinas, *Summa theologiae* IIIa, Q. 82, art. 3, quoted by the Office for the Liturgical Celebrations of the Supreme Pontiff: "Communion received on the tongue while kneeling" (2010).

[32] St Cyril of Jerusalem, *Mystagogical Catechesis* 5, 21ff. The communicant is to cup his hands, receive the Host in his *right* hand, and take the host with his mouth, using his hand as a paten.

[33] It was received either by intinction or by using a metal straw called a *fistula*.

Head-coverings

Something visible in many congregations attending the TLM, but much more rarely in the Novus Ordo, is the custom of women covering their heads, usually with a lace mantilla or "chapel veil."

This practice—an obligation of canon law under the 1917 *Code of Canon Law*, superseded by the 1983 *Code*—goes back to the primitive Church, together with the custom for men to uncover their heads. It has been rediscovered by many women whose interest in the Church's traditions has been piqued by their experience of the traditional Mass.

It is St Paul who insists, rather sharply, on this custom: "If anyone is inclined to dispute this, we have no other practice, nor do the churches of God."[34] So what, exactly, is its significance?

It is commonly said that the early Church adopted it in deference to local cultural norms, and this explanation has even found its way into official documents.[35] However, the practice St Paul describes does

---

[34] 1 Corinthians 11:16.
[35] Congregation for the Doctrine of the Faith, Instruction *Inter Insigniores* (1976).

not correspond to Greek, Roman, or Jewish habits.
Greek men and women alike sacrificed to the gods
with uncovered heads; Romans did so with covered
heads; and for the Jews, the covering of the head for
prayer, sacrifice, or in the presence of the divine, was
associated with men, not women, as it is to this day.[36]
To distinguish men and women, and have men take
off their head-coverings, and women keep theirs on,
seems if anything an inversion of Jewish practice, and
has nothing to do with the practice of the pagans of
St Paul's world.

We are forced, therefore, to take seriously the reasons St Paul himself gives for this practice, reasons
that continue to have meaning for us today. St Paul
connects his rationale for covering or uncovering
the head in the liturgy with the analogy of Christ as
the bridegroom of the Church, which he compares
with the relationship between the head and the body.
Christ is the head of the Church, and the Church's
human members make up the mystical Body of Christ.
This is analogous, St Paul tells us, to the human family,

---

[36] Orthodox Jewish men, in liturgical prayer, use a double head-
covering: the prayer-shawl (*shallit*) over the skull-cap (*yarmulke*).

in which the husband is the head, the wife (and other members of the family) the body. Christ loves the Church, and a husband should love his wife, as his own body, and "he is the saviour of his body." In both cases this self-sacrificial love corresponds to leadership, and should be reciprocated with respect (Eph 5:22–24).

Head-coverings come into this as a marker of subordination (1 Cor 11:10) and of holiness (1 Cor 12:23). It symbolises, therefore, the Church as the spotless bride, which the female members of the congregation represent. This idea was taken up by Pope John Paul II when he wrote of women having a "spousal character":[37]

> This spousal dimension, which is part of all consecrated life, has a particular meaning for women, who find therein their feminine identity and as it were discover the special genius of their relationship with the Lord.[38]

---

[37] Pope John Paul II, Apostolic Letter *Mulieris Dignitatem* (1988), no. 20.

[38] Pope John Paul II, Post-Synodal Apostolic Exhortation *Vita Consecrata* (1996), no. 34.

Women more readily represent the Church as bride, and men Christ the bridegroom—a fact obviously linked to the teaching of the Church that only men can be ordained as priests.

The theologian Manfred Hauke notes, having referred to the Blessed Virgin Mary as "archetype of 'Mother Church'":[39] "In an analogical way, therefore, women, too, are representative *and* embodiments of the Church. As opposed to men and the male priesthood, they symbolise a reality with which they are themselves identical."[40] Men symbolise the authority of Christ, to which they are themselves subject.

To what extent St Paul's theology of the Church as Bride of Christ can or should be disentangled from his teaching about authority in the household goes beyond the scope of this booklet: I can only urge readers to follow up the references to St Paul's letters, and look up the way his words have been understood by the Fathers and Doctors of the Church.

[39] Manfred Hauke, *Women in the Priesthood? A Systematic Analysis in the Light of the Order of Creation and Redemption* (San Francisco: Ignatius Press, 1986), 322.
[40] Hauke, 324; emphasis in the original.

What we can say is that for a woman to take up this custom, which goes back to the earliest days of the Church and is still maintained in the Eastern Churches, is to demonstrate the Church's spousal character in relation to Christ, in a way that the male members of the congregation cannot so easily do. This spousal character, in relation to Christ, is a matter of fidelity and holiness, since the Church, for all her human shortcomings, will be presented as a chaste virgin to Christ at the end of time (2 Cor 11:2), because she has been saved by Him.

Today, head-coverings are not part of mainstream fashion, and for women to cover their heads in church, particularly with a special head-covering not used in any other context, is an example of a phenomenon noted by Pope John Paul II: "the liturgy, though it must always be properly inculturated, must also be countercultural."[41] The countercultural nature of the gesture gives it heightened power to witness to the holiness of the liturgy, as a place where different rules apply.

---

[41] Pope John Paul II, Ad Limina Address to the Bishops of the Northwestern Region of the United States, October 9, 1998.

Male altar servers

The issue of women covering their heads in church leads naturally to the issue of only men and boys being allowed to serve at Mass in the TLM. They differ, however, is that while head-coverings are no longer an obligation deriving from the law of the Church, females are still excluded from serving in the traditional Mass by the law of the Church, as has been confirmed by the competent authorities in Rome. This is because the celebration of the traditional Mass is governed by the liturgical law contained in the 1962 *Missale Romanum*.[42]

Lay servers substitute for those formally given this task as acolytes, who can be men only, and are most often seminarians. This is true both under the old rules, when the role of acolyte was one of the "minor orders," and under the new rules, when the role of acolyte is an "instituted ministry." In the TLM, we can see that in Sung Mass with just one priest and lay servers, the servers perform many tasks allocated to the deacon and the subdeacon in Solemn (High) Mass.

---

[42] Pontifical Commission Ecclesia Dei, Instruction *Ecclesia Dei* (2010), nos. 24 and 28. The issue is dealt with in *De Defectibus* X, which is contained in the 1962 *Missale Romanum*.

Altar servers are related, then, to the priesthood, as a subordinate rung on a hierarchy reaching up to the priesthood, and as an intimate assistant of the priest in the celebration of Mass. The issue has special weight in the traditional Mass because the role of server is more complex and of greater importance, and while it is possible for a priest to celebrate Mass without a server, this is something that priests, and the faithful attached to the traditional Mass, seek to avoid. It is not unknown, in fact, for one priest to serve another priest's Mass, where others servers are unavailable, and the ability to serve Mass is very widespread among men who regularly attend the traditional Mass. In short, it is taken very seriously.

A parallel point can be made about other aspects of the traditional Mass that have already been discussed. We might say, about the reception of Holy Communion kneeling and on the tongue, that Catholics may believe in the Real Presence even without this practice, and this is true, but as Pope Benedict has already been quoted as saying, it marks it with "an exclamation point." The wearing of a head-covering by women at Mass is not a necessary underpinning for the Church's teaching on the complementarily of the sexes, but it certainly makes that teaching more visible. The celebration of Mass *ad orientem*, with a common direction of worship for priest and people, is not required for the teaching on the eschatological meaning of the Mass; nevertheless, as Christoph Cardinal Schönborn remarked, in a retreat preached to Pope John Paul II: "Yet how important such signs are for 'incarnating' the faith. The common prayer of priest and faithful *ad orientem* connected this cosmic 'orientation' with faith in the Resurrection of Christ, the *sol Invictus* [unconquered sun], and with His *Parousia* in glory."[43] In these ways, the traditional Mass makes the perennial teaching of the Church visible, audible, and dramatic, expressing it in memorable symbols.

This is why the ceremonies and prayers of the traditional Mass have value: because they express the beauty of the Faith. To mention some issues not already discussed, the priest's consistent acts of reverence towards the Blessed Sacrament on the Altar; his repeated prayers for purification; the visible preparation for Mass with the "Prayers at the Foot of the Altar"; the genuflection

---

[43] Christoph Cardinal Schönborn, *Loving the Church* (San Francisco: Ignatius Press, 1996), 205.

at the reference to the Incarnation in the Last Gospel: the realities that these things seek to express—the Real Presence, our sinfulness, the Incarnation—are things that we must hold with lively faith, for they are truths without which we cannot live in the Faith. To go beyond a merely intellectual assent to them, we need to meditate upon them, and let them enter into us. To quote again the words of Pope John Paul II, the liturgy can facilitate the "gradual identification with the mystery celebrated with one's whole person."

3

WHERE DID IT COME FROM?
The Organic Development of the Liturgy

In its discussion of liturgical reform, the Second Vatican Council's Constitution on the Liturgy, *Sacrosanctum Concilium*, demanded (among other things) that "care must be taken that any new forms adopted should in some way grow organically from forms already existing."[44] The phrase "organic development" is often used in discussions of the liturgy, and it will be useful to give some idea of how the liturgy has, in fact, developed through history.

It must first be noted how little we know of the earliest liturgy. The earliest liturgical books that have survived to the present day are from the seventh century. Into this gap of detailed knowledge it is very tempting for scholars to place what they would like to see, or to extend their favoured principles of development, such

---

[44] *Sacrosanctum Concilium*, no. 23.

as "the more complex derives from the less complex," backwards in time, without any real justification.

However, the Christian liturgy did not begin with a clean slate. It is based on three sources. The first is the Last Supper, which is connected to the liturgy by the Gospels and by St Paul. The Synoptic Gospels are clear that this was a Passover meal (e.g., Mt 26:17–19), which had its own ritual. The second is the liturgy of the Synagogue, in which Jesus and his disciples all took part (e.g., Lk 4:21), which consisted of readings from scripture, prayers, and teaching from a rabbi.

The third is the liturgy of the Temple, in which, again, our Lord and the disciples took part (e.g., Jn 7:14). This was the scene of complex ceremonial undertaken by a special class of priests and Levites, wearing special clothes, with a calendar of seasons and sacrifices, feasts and fasts, over the year. The importance of the Temple liturgy in the thinking of the earliest Christians is attested by the Letter to the Hebrews and the Apocalypse of St John. The letter places great stress on the sacrificial priest entering through the veil that separates the faithful from the Holy of Holies, and presents Christ the High Priest as accomplishing this passage definitively (see Heb 8–10 *et passim*). In the Apocalypse, the Temple's example lies behind the description of the liturgy of heaven, with its Altar, the sacrificed Lamb, clouds of incense, ritual exclamations, and prostrations (see Rev 7:9–12, 8:3, *et passim*).

While we don't know in any detail how the earliest liturgy was conducted, the liturgy we see recorded in the earliest liturgical books we *do* have combine these three influences. A number of features of later liturgy have not yet emerged in these books, but that does not mean the Mass they describe is simple; indeed, by then it may have been influenced by another source, the ceremonial of Imperial Rome. Certainly, when the time of persecution was over, Christians were quick to adopt the model of the civic meeting hall, the basilica (literally, "king's house"), for churches.

Analysis of literary style suggests that certain liturgical texts go back much further than the bound volumes in which they are preserved. The Roman Canon is generally regarded as having been composed (and not translated from a Greek original) at the end of the fourth century; the "Intercessions" (*Orationes sollemnes*) of the Good Friday Liturgy seem to be still older, echoing the language of St Clement of Rome,[45] who was Pope until his death in the year 99. The tone and content of these most ancient of liturgical texts anticipates the *gravitas* and the theological concerns of the traditional Mass as it is experienced today, and in which they are still found.

There were several kinds of process through which the liturgy developed.

In the early centuries, there was a great deal of liturgical variation between places, and the history of the liturgy is in large part a history of the mutual influence of different liturgical traditions. The Frankish Emperor Charlemagne (who died in 814), whose advisors included the scholar Alcuin of York, was concerned that errors had crept in to the liturgical texts and copies of the Bible in his dominions, and had the most highly-regarded books brought in from Rome, to be copied and used; expert singers were also brought in to pass on the Roman style of chant.

The liturgical volume Charlemagne was sent, a "Sacramentary" today known as the "Hadrianum," brought the liturgy of Rome to the whole of Christian France

---

[45] St Clement of Rome, *Ad Corinth.* (ca. AD 59–61).

and Germany, but it did not include everything that was needed, and so was supplemented by local, "Gallican," texts. This created a fusion of the Roman and Gallican traditions.

Later, in the tenth century, it was Rome where, for various reasons, the need was felt to correct and augment the liturgical books locally available with the best that could be found elsewhere. This was a volume known as the "Romano-Germanic Pontifical," which came from Metz. This served to bring texts of non-Roman origin into the Roman tradition.

On a smaller scale, ceremonies or texts that were well-established in one location could be incorporated into the liturgy of another. The freedom with which this could happen is illustrated by advice given by Pope Gregory the Great to St Augustine of Canterbury, about what liturgical books to use in England, where he had arrived in the year 597: "Select from the Churches whatever things are devout, religious, and right; and when you have bound them, as it were, into a sheaf, let the minds of the English grow accustomed to it."[46]

---

[46] Quoted in Alcuin Reid, *The Organic Development of the Liturgy* (San Francisco: Ignatius Press, 2005), 20ff.

In a similar way, texts and ceremonies once used only in a restricted context could be used in a wider context. An example is the Gloria, originally specific to Christmas, but later used for joyful feasts throughout the year, and on Sundays outside Advent and Lent.

In these ways, there was a mutual influence among different liturgical rites and usages in the West, and sometimes also influences from the East, as with the adoption of the feasts of Candlemas and the Transfiguration. This kind of development was a matter of supplementing or replacing one's local books with things of great prestige from elsewhere.

Some other processes of liturgical development should also be mentioned. One is that when new circumstances demanded it, new or adapted texts and ceremonies would be adopted. An example would be the development of the Christian monarchies, which led to the development of coronation liturgies. Another developing need was the increasing desire of the faithful to see the Blessed Sacrament during the Consecration, which led to the development of the Elevation. Another kind of need derived from the problems experienced with the most ancient form of the Kiss of Peace, which led to the development of the Paxbrede (an object which is kissed, by the celebrant and then by each member of the congregation in turn),[47] and later the restriction of the Kiss to those in the sanctuary.

In these ways the liturgy adapted to the evolving circumstances of the times. It did so also in another way: in relation to the liturgical resources available. For example, in the ninth century, Low Mass—Mass celebrated by a priest alone, without deacon or subdeacon—developed for situations in which those assistants were not always available, notably when priests in monasteries, and later in parishes, wished to celebrate a daily Mass. Without the deacon or subdeacon, the ceremonies had to be quite drastically cut down. By contrast, in cathedrals the abundance of available clergy and singers led to the development of ceremonies involving more and more of them.

In a similar way, St Francis of Assisi decided to adopt the liturgy of the Papal Court for his own order. This implied a degree of adaptation to the circumstances

---

[47] Today the Paxbrede is still used in the Extraordinary Form for the congregation in Spain and its former dominions, and in some religious orders for the clergy, notably in the traditional Dominican Rite.

the Friars would find themselves in all over Christendom. The extremely happy result of this adaptation, the thirteenth century "*Missale Romano-Seraphicum*," is the direct ancestor of the traditional Mass as celebrated today: a version of the papal liturgy that can be celebrated in parish churches, on battlefields and on missions, as well as in great cathedrals.

These forms of liturgical development are essentially conservative in nature, the driving force being the authenticity, antiquity, and prestige of ceremonies and texts being adopted by one tradition from another. Even when new or adapted texts and ceremonies were needed, they took their inspiration from existing precedents. Thus Christian kings from the early Middle Ages onwards were anointed like the kings of the Old Testament. Where brevity and simplicity were demanded for practical reasons, the fuller and more complex ceremony would often be alluded to, or included in symbolic, telescoped form. At Low Mass there is no deacon and subdeacon to receive the celebrant's blessing and carry the Gospel solemnly, with candles and incense, across the sanctuary, to be proclaimed towards the north, symbol of the yet-unconverted world: yet the priest uses almost the same words to ask God's blessing, and the Missal is transferred with some ceremony from the south to the north end of the Altar by the server, where it is placed at an angle to face a little towards the north, rather that directly towards liturgical east.

Over time, the prestige of the Roman liturgy itself led to the spread of the Roman Rite at the expense of local rites and usages. The adoption of the Roman Rite by the Franciscans was a key moment in this process: from then on, the Roman Rite was to be heard all over Europe. The historical and cultural importance of local rites was not entirely neglected, however. More than once the people of Milan successfully opposed attempts to suppress their own venerable "Ambrosian" Rite (named after St Ambrose of Milan); the "Mozarabic" Rite of Spain was carefully preserved, if only for use in two locations; and many of the great religious orders preserved their own liturgical books: the Dominicans, the Norbertines, the Carmelites, and the Cistercians. Pope Pius V, in his Bull *Quo Primum* (1570), demanded that local usages of any real age— two hundred years or more—should continue to be followed unless the Cathedral Chapter (or the General Chapter of a religious order) and the bishop (or superior) both agreed to adopt the Roman Rite. The Gallican Rites of France, the various rites of the British Isles, and the rites of Germany, eventually ceased to be used, but this was an extremely slow process, complete only in the mid- to late nineteenth century.

Although the different Missals used in the Western Church have a great deal in common, at the eve of the Second Vatican Council the Western Church was not characterised by uniformity in liturgical matters, to say nothing of the Eastern Rites, which were celebrated wherever Eastern clergy and faithful were to be found.

The Council of Trent ordered a careful examination of the Roman books, with a view to their correction. Missals from the fourteenth and fifteenth centuries were duly consulted and where texts had been corrupted, they were restored to their original form.

At Trent, the use of Latin and the ceremonies of the Catholic liturgy were defended with great eloquence against Protestant objections. Notably, the Council Fathers taught:

> And whereas such is the nature of man, that, without external helps, he cannot easily be raised to the meditation of divine things;

therefore has holy Mother Church instituted certain rites, to wit that certain things be pronounced in the Mass in a low, and others in a louder, tone. She has likewise employed ceremonies, such as mystic benedictions, lights, incense, vestments, and many other things of this kind, derived from an apostolical discipline and tradition, whereby both the majesty of so great a sacrifice might be recommended, and the minds of the faithful be excited, by those visible signs of religion and piety, to the contemplation of those most sublime things which are hidden in this sacrifice.[48]

The errors opposed by Trent again became an issue in the seventeenth and eighteenth centuries, with attempts, influenced by the Jansenist heresy, to create an "Enlightenment" liturgy, in the vernacular, with simplified ceremonies, no silence, and the people saying "Amen" after each prayer of the Canon. This took its most comprehensive form under the Emperor Joseph II of Austria (1741–1790), whose liturgical

---

[48] Council of Trent, Session 22, Chapter V (1562).

innovations (which lacked any authorisation from the Holy See) were accompanied by a ferocious persecution of the contemplative religious orders in his domains. It was during this era, also, that the Jesuits, who were among the most effective opponents of this project, were expelled from many countries, and even suppressed by Pope Clement VIII in 1773, under intense pressure from supposedly Catholic monarchs.

In one of the great ironies of history, the era of the "Enlightened Despots" who had caused the Church such grief was brought to an end by Napoleon, and his eventual defeat. This ushered in a period of unprecedented restoration, of church buildings, Catholic schools, and monasticism, with a renewed interest in the Church's liturgy, leading to the studies of the "Liturgical Movement," and the revival of Gregorian chant. Even the Jesuits were revived, in 1814.

4

What Is It For?

The Place of the Traditional Mass in the Church

Liturgical and spiritual pluralism

There is no intrinsic problem about the Church as a whole, or the Western Church in particular, having multiple liturgical forms. This has been the norm throughout history, and as the Second Vatican Council taught: "Even in the liturgy, the Church has no wish to impose a rigid uniformity in matters which do not implicate the faith or the good of the whole community."[49] Nevertheless, any liturgical form that enjoys a place in the life of the Church is justified in terms of how it contributes to the Church's mission of saving souls and glorifying God. If it brings people to Faith, and strengthens and sustains those already there, then there can be no objection to it. That the traditional Mass does exactly this is indicated in the words of Pope Benedict: there are

---

[49] *Sacrosanctum Concilium*, no. 37.

those who find the traditional Mass "particularly suited to them"; more simply still, this rite represents "riches" that the Church should treasure.[50] A partial parallel can be seen in the relationship between the liturgies of the West and of the East. The Second Vatican Council's decree on Ecumenism explained:

> In the study of revelation East and West have followed different methods, and have developed differently their understanding and confession of God's truth. It is hardly surprising, then, if from time to time one tradition has come nearer to a full appreciation of some aspects of a mystery of revelation than the other, or has expressed it to better advantage. In such cases, these various theological expressions are to be considered often as mutually complementary rather than conflicting.[51]

In a similar way, the things that the traditional Mass can teach us take nothing away from the Novus Ordo.

---

[50] Pope Benedict XVI, *Con Grande Fiducia*, letter to bishops accompanying *Summorum Pontificum* (2007).

[51] *Unitatis Redintegratio*, no. 17.

The doctrinal wealth and spiritual tradition represented by the traditional Mass are, after all, simply those of the Catholic Church from ancient times to the mid-1960s, and this cannot be said to be in conflict with the teaching of the Church today. In the words of Pope Benedict, already quoted: "Let us generously open our hearts and make room for everything that the faith itself allows."

Who is attracted to the traditional Mass?

Why should anyone gain particular insight or inspiration from the traditional Mass? The outlines of an answer to this question have already been given in the opening chapter of this booklet. The TLM communicates with the worshipper in a way somewhat distinct from the mode employed by the Novus Ordo. Whereas the latter primarily uses words, the TLM uses a wide range of means, with greater emphasis on dramatic ceremonial and the creation of a sense of the sacred: "the sacrality which attracts many people" to it, as Pope Benedict noted.[52] The way that the traditional Mass conveys the sense of the sacred non-verbally can be

---

[52] *Con Grande Fiducia.*

particularly useful to those for whom the words of the liturgy are less effective at conveying the mystery of the Mass. Most obviously, this will include those less at ease with the language in which the Novus Ordo is celebrated, such as people who hear Mass being celebrated in a second language, children, and males.

To consider these groups in reverse order, it has been shown that men are less verbally-oriented than women, and a very striking feature of the traditional Mass is that whereas in Britain and America men make up only about one in three of the typical Catholic congregation, in the traditional Mass congregations are typically slightly more than 50 percent men.

Small children seem to appreciate the atmosphere of the traditional Mass, and while evidence is only anecdotal, it is often said that even children not used to it are quieter and more recollected at a Mass that is itself quieter, and where there is an atmosphere of quiet for them to absorb and imitate. "Children's liturgies" are not felt to be necessary at celebrations of the traditional Mass, and many congregations include an unusually large number of children.

Those obliged to hear Mass in a second language, or perhaps one not understood at all, will not reap the advantages offered by the Novus Ordo in terms of the immediate comprehension of the texts. This is true not only of many immigrants, but also of native speakers of minority languages—a serious obstacle to a truly "vernacular" liturgy, particularly in Africa and China. These Catholics may also be attracted to the traditional Mass because its spirituality is more akin to the traditional spirituality of many cultures. This affinity has also been expressed by Jewish and Muslim converts, who are used to a more atmospheric, ritualised, form of worship, with the use of sacred languages and chant.

In a somewhat different way, the TLM has also on occasion had a special appeal to those attracted to the New Age, who, as the late Stratford Caldecott expressed it, seek "a *transforming contact* with mystery."[53] Anyone put off by a rationalistic presentation of religion will find, in the traditional Mass (to repeat the words of Pope Benedict), "a form of encounter with the Mystery of the Most Holy Eucharist, particularly suited to them."

---

[53] Stratford Caldecott, *Understanding the New Age* (London: Catholic Truth Society, 2006), 51.

CONCLUSION

Feedback from two recent events for young professionals in London, which included the celebration of a Sung Mass in the traditional Mass of the Roman Rite, in one case, and of the traditional Dominican Rite (very similar to the TLM), in the other, supply some anecdotal evidence for how this liturgical tradition appears to people new to it.

Not everyone liked it, but those who felt motivated to use a feedback form to say so were few. The great majority recorded a positive response: the words "solemn," "beautiful," "reverent," and "prayerful" predominate. Others commented "A charming experience," and "So calm and pure." One wrote: "I feel so blessed to be able to see such a reverent Rite for Our Lord."

The Diocese of Miami, Florida, records a story on its website about a young woman whose experience of the traditional Mass on a visit to England helped her find the Catholic Church.

Formerly an atheist, her aversion toward religion changed at the end of her college career,
when she became a Protestant. During her
post-collegiate travels she became resolute
in converting to Catholicism after attending
a *Missa Cantata*, or sung Mass, in the parish of
her favourite author, J.R.R. Tolkien, a devout
Catholic who penned *The Lord of the Rings*
series. . . . When she heard Latin hymns coming from the choir loft, Tavakoli said, it felt like
"hearing angels on high." She was mesmerized.
"It truly is extraordinary," she said. "There is
something beautiful and sacred about this
form of the Mass."[54]

Longstanding members of the movement in support
of the traditional Mass know many such stories. Sometimes this Mass can reach people in a special way. The
movement is not about forcing people to attend a Mass
that does not suit them: it is about making possible a
spiritual experience that some find helpful, and others
life-changing.

---

[54] www.miamiarch.org/CatholicDiocese.php?op=Article_137
23162813374.

When attending the traditional Mass, we can consider its central place not just in the history, art, and culture of the Church, but in her spirituality, which goes beyond the reality of sacrament and sacrifice that all valid Eucharistic liturgies have in common. The prayers and ceremonies, the Latin and silence that clothe the Eucharist in this liturgy act as a guide to our spiritual participation in it. It was with this way of celebrating Mass in mind that, to give just one example, the "Apostle of the Eucharist" St. Peter Julian Eymard wrote: "Know, O Christian, that the Mass is the holiest act of religion. You cannot do anything to glorify God more, nor profit your soul more, than by devoutly assisting at it, and assisting as often as possible." As Pope Benedict XVI remarked, the traditional Mass represents great "riches" for the Church. These are riches of which no Catholic of the Latin rite should be deprived.

Further Reading
and Resources

How to find a Latin Mass

A number of websites exist that specialize in collating information on the churches that offer the traditional Mass. Three prominent ones are:

www.latinmass.com

www.latinmassdir.org

www.latinritemass.net

Learning more through video

The "Mass of the Ages" videos, viewed by millions, are a helpful way not only to learn more about the liturgy but also to introduce others who may not be inclined to read a book or pamphlet. See:

❖ Episode 1: Discover the Latin Mass

❖ Episode 2: A Perfect Storm

At time of printing, Episode 3 is under development.

www.latinmass.com

Short guides through the Mass

- Lisa Bergman, *Treasure and Tradition: The Ultimate Guide to the Latin Mass* (St. Augustine Academy Press, 2014)
- Fr. Thomas Crean, *The Mass and the Saints* (Ignatius Press, 2009)
- Dom Prosper Guéranger, *The Traditional Latin Mass Explained* (Angelico Press, 2017)
- Msgr. Ronald Knox, *The Mass in Slow Motion* (1948; reprinted by Cluny Media, 2022)
- Derya Little, *A Beginner's Guide to the Traditional Latin Mass* (Angelico Press, 2019)
- Msgr. George J. Moorman, *The Latin Mass Explained* (TAN Books, 2007)

Hand missals

- *Daily Missal 1962* (Baronius Press)
- *1962 Roman Catholic Daily Missal* (Angelus Press)
- *St Andrew Daily Missal 1945* (St Bonaventure Publications)
- *The New Roman Missal* (1945) (Christian Book Club of America)
- *A Missal for Young Catholics* (Os Justi Press)

❖ *Benedictus* (monthly subscription, with devotions and meditations)

Also recommended: *The Illustrated Liturgical Year* (Sophia Institute Press)

On liturgy in general

❖ Joseph Ratzinger, *The Spirit of the Liturgy* (Ignatius Press, 2000; reprinted, together with Romano Guardini's work of the same name, in 2018)

❖ Athanasius Schneider, *The Catholic Mass: Steps to Restore the Centrality of God in the Liturgy* (Sophia Institute Press, 2022)

❖ Joseph Shaw, *The Liturgy, the Family, and the Crisis of Modernity* (Os Justi Press, 2023)

In-depth treatments of the TLM

❖ Fr. Claude Barthe, *A Forest of Symbols: The Traditional Mass and Its Meaning* (Angelico Press, 2023)

❖ Michael Fiedrowicz, *The Traditional Mass: History, Form, and Theology of the Classical Roman Rite* (Angelico Press, 2020)

❖ Peter Kwasniewski, *The Once and Future Roman Rite: Returning to the Traditional Latin Liturgy after Seventy Years of Exile* (TAN Books, 2022)

- Peter Kwasniewski, *Reclaiming Our Roman Catholic Birthright: The Genius and Timeliness of the Traditional Latin Mass* (Angelico Press, 2020)
- St. Leonard of Port Maurice, *The Hidden Treasure: Holy Mass* (TAN Books, 2012)
- Martin Mosebach, *The Heresy of Formlessness: The Roman Liturgy and Its Enemy* (Angelico Press, 2018)
- Joseph Shaw, ed., *The Case for Liturgical Restoration: Una Voce Studies on the Traditional Latin Mass* (Angelico Press, 2019)
- Martin von Cochem, *The Incredible Catholic Mass* (TAN Books, 2012)

On the liturgical reform

- Yves Chiron, *Annibale Bugnini: Reformer of the Liturgy* (Angelico Press, 2018)
- Michael Davies, *Cranmer's Godly Order: The Destruction of Catholicism through Liturgical Change* (Roman Catholic Books, 1995)
- Michael Davies, *Pope Paul's New Mass* (1980; reprinted by Angelus Press, 2009)
- Fr. Klaus Gamber, *The Reform of the Roman Liturgy: Its Problems and Background* (Una Voce Press, 1993)

❖ Peter Kwasniewski, ed., *Illusions of Reform: Responses to Cavadini, Healy, and Weinandy in Defense of the Traditional Mass and the Faithful Who Attend It* (Os Justi Press, 2023)

Specific issues

❖ Stuart Chessman, *Faith of Our Fathers: A Brief History of Catholic Traditionalism in the United States, from Triumph to Traditionis Custodes* (Angelico Press, 2022)

❖ Matthew Hazell, *Index Lectionum: A Comparative Table of Readings for the Ordinary and Extraordinary Form of the Roman Rite* (2016)

❖ Peter A. Kwasniewski, *True Obedience in the Church: A Guide to Discernment in Challenging Times* (Sophia Institute Press, 2021)

❖ Bishop Juan Rodolfo Laise, *Communion in the Hand* (Preserving Christian Publications, 2011; rev. ed., 2018)

❖ Fr. Uwe Michael Lang, *Turning Towards the Lord: Orientation in Liturgical Prayer* (Ignatius Press, 2009)

❖ Christine Mohrmann, *Liturgical Latin: Its Origins and Character* (1959; repr. by various)

❖ Lauren Pristas, *The Collects of the Roman Missals* (T & T Clark, 2013)

❖ Roberto Spataro, *In Praise of the Tridentine Mass and of Latin, Language of the Church* (Angelico Press, 2019)

Fiction

* Fr. Bryan Houghton, *Mitre and Crook* (1979; reprinted by Angelico Press, 2019)
* Fr. Bryan Houghton, *Judith's Marriage* (1987; reprinted by Angelico Press, 2020)
* Michael Kent, *The Mass of Brother Michel* (1942; reprinted by Angelico Press, 2017)

Other sacraments

It is natural that those attached to the traditional Mass should seek the other sacraments in this form, as the ceremonies and prayers are very much in the same spirit. For example, the Nuptial Blessing in the TLM Wedding Service is a long and very beautiful prayer invoking a succession of blessings, specifically for the bride, who in the Pauline conception of marriage noted earlier is the "body" of the husband and represents the family. Similarly, in the baptismal ceremony of the traditional Mass, there is a succession of exorcisms recalling the exorcisms used in the early Church for converts from paganism, together with vivid and dramatic rituals: the giving to the candidate of a tiny portion of salt, representing wisdom, and the opening of the candidate's ears and mouth, recalling our Lord's cure of the deaf and dumb man (Mk 7:33), and even the use of the same Aramaic word of command: *ephphatha*. The ceremony of the rite of Confirmation, which is short, includes the vivid symbolic striking of each candidate's cheek by the bishop, recalling the *colée* of the medieval knighting ceremony.

⁜ Traditional Baptism: www.latinmassbaptism.com
⁜ Traditional Confirmation: www.latinmassconfirma-tion.com
⁜ Traditional Wedding: www.latinmasswedding.com
⁜ Traditional Funeral: www.latinmassfuneral.com

More online resources

⁜ Catholic Family News—www.catholicfamilynews.com
⁜ Catholic Music Association of America—www.musicasacra.com
⁜ Corpus Christi Watershed—www.ccwatershed.org
⁜ The Divinum Officium Project—www.divinumof-ficium.com
⁜ Foederatio Internationalis Una Voce (Una Voce International)—www.fiuv.org
⁜ Foederatio Internationalis Juventutem (youth move-ment)—www.juventutem.org
⁜ Fisheaters: The Whys and Hows of Traditional Catholicism—www.fisheaters.com

❖ Latin Mass Magazine—www.latinmassmagazine.com

❖ LiveMass (many TLMs broadcast per day)—www.
   livemass.net

❖ New Liturgical Movement—www.newliturgical
   movement.org

❖ OnePeterFive—https://onepeterfive.com

❖ Online Liturgical Ordo—https://propria.org

❖ Thesaurus Preces Latinae—www.preces-latinae.org/
   index.htm

❖ Liturgy of the Home—https://www.liturgyofthe
   home.com

Smartphone apps

❖ iMass

❖ iPieta (TLM and NOM calendars and readings for
   Mass, and many other resources)

❖ Liber Pro (searchable scan of the *Liber Usualis*)

❖ Vetus Ordo Missae App

Made in United States
Orlando, FL
16 July 2024

49042688R00055